Junior Drug Awareness

Amphetamines
& Other Uppers

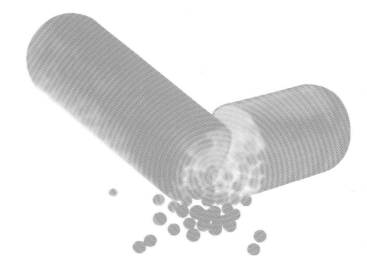

Junior Drug Awareness

Junior Drug Awareness

Amphetamines
& Other Uppers

Introduction by **BARRY R. McCAFFREY**
Director, Office of National Drug Control Policy

Foreword by **STEVEN L. JAFFE, M.D.**
Senior Consulting Editor,
Professor of Child and Adolescent Psychiatry, Emory University

Linda N. Bayer, Ph.D.

Chelsea House Publishers
Philadelphia

*The author wishes to dedicate this book to her mother, **Lillian Bayer Marlow**, who has all the energy, drive, and concern for young people that anyone could want. Would that all children and grandchildren could benefit from knowing a woman of valor like her.*

CHELSEA HOUSE PUBLISHERS
Editor in Chief Stephen Reginald
Production Manager Pamela Loos
Director of Photography Judy L. Hasday
Art Director Sara Davis
Managing Editor James D. Gallagher
Senior Production Editor LeeAnne Gelletly

Staff for AMPHETAMINES
Senior Editor Therese De Angelis
Associate Art Director Takeshi Takahashi
Picture Researcher Patricia Burns
Designer Keith Trego
Cover Illustrator/Designer Keith Trego

Cover photo PhotoDisc, Vol. 45 #45110

The Chelsea House World Wide Web site address is
http://www.chelseahouse.com

3 5 7 9 8 6 4 2

Library of Congress Cataloging-in-Publication Data

Bayer, Linda N.
Amphetamines and other uppers / Linda N. Bayer.
80 pp.   cm. — (Junior drug awareness series)
Includes bibliographical references and index.
Summary: Discusses the history of amphetamines, describes the effects of stimulants on the body, and offers advice on recognizing abuse and getting help.
ISBN 0-7910-5200-1 (hc)
1. Amphetamine abuse—Juvenile literature. 2. Amphet-amines—Juvenile literature. [1. Amphetamines. 2. Drug abuse.] I. Title. II. Series: Junior drug awareness.
RC568.A45B39 1999
616.86'4—dc21   99-17916
                                                              CIP
                                                              AC

CONTENTS

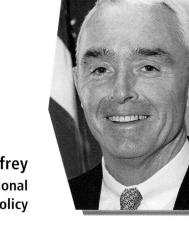

by Barry R. McCaffrey
Director, Office of National
Drug Control Policy

STAYING AWAY FROM ILLEGAL DRUGS, TOBACCO PRODUCTS, AND ALCOHOL

G ood health allows you to be as strong, happy, smart, and skillful as you can possibly be. The worst thing about illegal drugs is that they damage people from the inside. Our bodies and minds are wonderful, complicated systems that run like finely tuned machines when we take care of ourselves.

Doctors prescribe legal drugs, called medicines, to heal us when we become sick, but dangerous chemicals that are not recommended by doctors, nurses, or pharmacists are called illegal drugs. These drugs cannot be bought in stores because they harm different organs of the body, causing illness or even death. Illegal drugs, such as marijuana, cocaine or "crack," heroin, methamphetamine ("meth"), and other dangerous substances are against the law because they affect our ability to think, work, play, sleep, or eat.

If anyone ever offers you illegal drugs or any kind of pills, liquids, substances to smoke, or shots to inject into your body, tell them you're not interested. You should report drug pushers—people who distribute these poisons—to parents, teachers, police, coaches, clergy, or other adults whom you trust.

Cigarettes and alcohol are also illegal for youngsters. Tobacco products and drinks like wine, beer, and liquor are particularly harmful for children and teenagers because their bodies, especially their nervous systems, are still developing. For this reason, young people are more likely to be hurt by illicit drugs—including cigarettes and alcohol. These two products kill more people—from cancer, and automobile accidents caused by intoxicated drivers—than all other drugs combined. We say about drug use: "Users are losers." Be a winner and stay away from illegal drugs, tobacco products, and alcoholic beverages.

Here are four reasons why you shouldn't use illegal drugs:

- Illegal drugs can cause brain damage.
- Illegal drugs are "psychoactive." This means that they change your personality or the way you feel. They also impair your judgment. While under the influence of drugs, you are more likely to endanger your life or someone else's. You will also be less able to protect yourself from danger.
- Many illegal drugs are addictive, which means that once a person starts taking them, stopping is extremely difficult. An addict's body craves the drug and becomes dependent upon it. The illegal drug–user may become sick if the drug is discontinued and so may become a slave to drugs.

- Some drugs, called "gateway" substances, can lead a person to take more-dangerous drugs. For example, a 12-year-old who smokes marijuana is 79 times more likely to have an addiction problem later in life than a child who never tries marijuana.

Here are some reasons why you shouldn't drink alcoholic beverages, including beer and wine coolers:

- Alcohol is the second leading cause of death in our country. More than 100,000 people die every year because of drinking.
- Adolescents are twice as likely as adults to be involved in fatal alcohol-related car crashes.
- Half of all assaults against girls or women involve alcohol.
- Drinking is illegal if you are under the age of 21. You could be arrested for this crime.

Here are three reasons why you shouldn't smoke cigarettes:

- Nicotine is highly addictive. Once you start smoking, it is very hard to stop, and smoking cigarettes causes lung cancer and other diseases. Tobacco- and nicotine-related diseases kill more than 400,000 people every year.
- Each day, 3,000 kids begin smoking. One-third of these youngsters will probably have their lives shortened because of tobacco use.
- Children who smoke cigarettes are almost six times more likely to use other illegal drugs than kids who don't smoke.

If your parents haven't told you how they feel about the dangers of illegal drugs, ask them. One of every 10 kids aged 12 to 17 is using illegal drugs. They do not understand the risks they are taking with their health and their lives. However, the vast majority of young people in America are smart enough to figure out that drugs, cigarettes, and alcohol could rob them of their future. Be your body's best friend: guard your mental and physical health by staying away from drugs.

WHY SHOULD I LEARN ABOUT DRUGS?

Steven L. Jaffe, M.D., Senior Consulting Editor,
Professor of Child and Adolescent Psychiatry,
Emory University

Your grandparents and great-grandparents did not think much about "drug awareness." That's because drugs, to most of them, simply meant "medicine."

Of the three types of drugs, medicine is the good type. Medicines such as penicillin and aspirin promote healing and help sick people get better.

Another type of drug is obviously bad for you because it is poison. Then there are the kinds of drugs that fool you, such as marijuana and LSD. They make you feel good, but they harm your body and brain.

Our great crisis today is that this third category of drugs has become widely abused. Drugs of abuse are everywhere, not just in rough neighborhoods. Many teens are introduced to drugs by older brothers, sisters, friends, or even friends' parents. Some people may use only a little bit of a drug, but others who inherited a tendency to become addicted may move on to using drugs all the time. If a family member is or was an alcoholic or an addict, a young person is at greater risk of becoming one.

Drug abuse can weaken us physically. Worse, it can cause permanent mental damage. Our brain is the most important part of our body. Our thoughts, hopes, wishes, feelings, and memories are located there, within 100 billion nerve cells. Alcohol and drugs that are abused will harm—and even destroy—these cells. During the teen years, your brain continues to develop and grow, but drugs and alcohol can impair this growth.

I treat all types of teenagers at my hospital programs and in my office. Many suffer from depression or anxiety. A lot of them abuse drugs and alcohol, and this makes their depression or fears worse. I have celebrated birthdays and high school graduations with many of my patients. But I have also been to sad funerals for others who have died from problems with drug abuse.

Doctors understand more about drugs today than ever before. We've learned that some substances (even some foods) that we once thought were harmless can actually cause health problems. And for some people, medicines that help relieve one symptom might cause problems in other ways. This is because each person's body chemistry and immune system are different.

For all of these reasons, drug awareness is important for everyone. We need to learn which drugs to avoid or question—not only the destructive, illegal drugs we hear so much about in the news, but also ordinary medicines we buy at the supermarket or pharmacy. We need to understand that even "good" drugs can hurt us if they are not used correctly. If we take any drug without a doctor's advice, we are taking a risk.

Drug awareness enables you to make good decisions. It allows you to become powerful and strong and have a meaningful life!

Amphetamines not only harm the user's body, but they can also cause paranoia and hallucinations—and may lead the user to commit acts of violence.

"SPEED KILLS"

A young woman who had taken **methamphetamine** arrived in the emergency room of her local hospital. She was so frantic and frightened that she thrashed about until she was sedated. Throughout the ordeal, she kept screaming, "Give me back my brain. I'm dying. I don't want to die without my brain."

In July 1995 in New Mexico, a man named Eric Smith, who was under the influence of methamphetamine, decapitated his 14-year-old son and threw the boy's head out the window of his van. The drug-crazed father thought he was getting rid of a demon.

A soldier who was depressed attempted suicide by taking an overdose of **amphetamines**. He was admitted to a hospital in a dazed condition with a severe headache and a slow pulse. That night his right arm and leg became paralyzed, and he developed difficulty breathing. Toward morning he vomited, his pulse rate increased, and his temperature reached almost 104 degrees. The man was given oxygen, sodium benzoate, and other substances, but he died just before 5:00 A.M. An autopsy (examination of the body after death) revealed that he had died from heavy and uncontrollable bleeding in the brain.

What Are Amphetamines?

The chemicals called amphetamine, **dextroamphetamine**, and methamphetamine are collectively called amphetamines. These drugs can be taken in various ways: swallowed in pill form, dissolved in a liquid, snorted through the nose, smoked, or injected **intravenously** (through the veins with a hypodermic needle). Some users of amphetamines want to get "high" or stay awake for long periods of time. Others use them to lose weight, since they reduce one's appetite and increase activity.

Some types of amphetamine can be prescribed in pill form by doctors to treat medical problems. Patients who may benefit from amphetamine prescriptions include those who suffer from obesity (extreme overweight), narcolepsy (a condition in which a person falls asleep uncontrollably during daytime hours), and attention deficit disorder, or ADD, which is characterized by a short attention span and **hyperactivity** (excessive activity). When sold or used for nonmedical purposes, however—to get high, for example—amphetamines are not only against the law but are also extremely dangerous.

Amphetamines are part of a category of drugs some-

Despite what you may believe, nicotine (found in all tobacco products) is a highly addictive stimulant. When you smoke cigarettes, you are actually using a drug.

times referred to as **stimulants**, "uppers," or "speed" because they speed up, or stimulate, the body's functions and increase the activity of the brain. These effects make users feel energetic, alert, and talkative. But as you can see from the stories you just read about people who have taken strong stimulants, they can be extremely dangerous—even deadly.

Some stimulants are not as powerful or as harmful as amphetamines. In fact, many people use them daily. Have you eaten a chocolate bar or had a soda recently? If so, you probably gave your body a dose of a mild stimulant—**caffeine**, which is also found in coffee, tea, and some over-the-counter medicines. Taken in small doses, caffeine is not harmful to most people. But because it

Most amphetamine abusers do not know that they have taken a toxic amount of the drug until it is too late. In the first half of 1996, DAWN (the Drug Abuse Warning Network) reported 1,595 emergency-room visits and 660 overdoses related to stimulant abuse in the United States.

can cause nervousness, agitation, or **insomnia** (inability to sleep), manufacturers of over-the-counter medicines and beverages containing caffeine usually offer consumers caffeine-free products as well.

Another stimulant that is probably familiar to you is **nicotine**, which is found in all tobacco products. You may not think of nicotine as a drug, but it is. Like most stimulants, nicotine is highly **addictive**, which means that once the body is exposed to the substance, it becomes dependent on the drug to function normally.

And as you know, smoking cigarettes or using chewing tobacco can also cause cancer and other deadly diseases such as emphysema (a heart and lung disorder).

Dangerous Stimulants

There are other forms of strong stimulants that are as dangerous as amphetamines. Some of the most common ones are:

- Cocaine—Made from the leaf of the coca plant, this illegal drug usually comes in the form of a white powder that is inhaled through the nose.
- Crack—A highly addictive solid form of cocaine, made by mixing the drug with other substances and then heating and hardening it. These small pieces, called "rocks," are smoked in a small pipe.
- Methamphetamine—A powerful form of amphetamine that is smoked or melted and taken intravenously. Methamphetamine comes in powder form (called "crank") or in clear crystals (called "ice" or "crystal meth").
- Ephedrine—Derived from the ephedra plant, ephedrine has been used for centuries as a safe and effective drug for treating asthma. When used without medical supervision or in high doses, however, it causes the same physical side effects as other strong stimulants. Despite their dangers, ephedrine tablets can be sold legally as "white crosses," "mini-thins," or "Magnum 357s" because they are mixed with other substances and marketed as asthma

remedies. The drug is also sold as a loose herb or tea preparation and incorrectly advertised as a "safe" alternative to **Ecstasy** (a combination of methamphetamine and a **hallucinogen** called MDA).

Why Are Amphetamines and Other Stimulants Dangerous?

Abusing amphetamines can lead to overdose or death from heart attack, stroke, or an extreme rise in body temperature. An amphetamine abuser rarely knows the dose he or she is taking, and it is common for users to keep taking the drug until they feel unpleasant side effects. But by then, it may be too late—the drug may have already reached **toxic** (poisonous) levels in the body.

After injecting, smoking, or snorting speed, the user feels a sudden sensation known as a "rush" or "flash." With large doses of stimulants, side effects can include dizziness, tremors (uncontrollable shaking), severe headaches, excessive sweating, chest pains, heart palpitations, flushed skin color, nausea, vomiting, and abdominal cramps. An amphetamine abuser may also become extremely agitated or even violent and may feel **paranoia** (unreasonable fear). High doses of amphetamines can produce terrifying visual or auditory **hallucinations**, meaning that users see and hear imaginary things as though they were real or experience distorted perceptions of reality. They may pick at imaginary insects under the skin called "crank bugs" until they develop wounds, which may become infected.

Like other stimulants, cocaine (shown here) increases the heart rate and blood pressure and expands the breathing tubes of the lungs. An overdose can produce convulsions, coma, or death.

Amphetamine abusers will become preoccupied with their own thoughts and actions. They may repeat the same word or phrase over and over or repeatedly assemble and take apart equipment such as a watch. People under the influence of amphetamines may also speak very rapidly for long periods of time. While under the influence of the drug, users can become so aggressive that they endanger their own lives and the lives of others. They are also typically unable to evaluate and avoid dangerous situations, and they are often involved in driving accidents and other mishaps. **Chronic** (continuous) abuse may cause a type of **psychosis**, a severe mental illness in which a person loses contact with reality.

A "speed freak" who overdoses will run a very high fever, experience convulsions, and possibly suffer from **cardiovascular** collapse. Immediate medical attention is necessary to keep the person alive. Physical exertion or combining amphetamines with other drugs makes the possibility of accidental death even more likely.

As with all addictive drugs, heavy users of amphetamine will develop a **tolerance** for the drug, which means that they have to take more and more of it to get the same sense of **euphoria** (an intense feeling of well-being) they once got with a smaller dose. Amphetamine abusers quickly become physically and psychologically dependent on the drug. They may **binge**, or indulge excessively over a brief period of time, taking the drug every few hours for days or even weeks. When the drug's effects wear off, the abuser "crashes." The person feels exhausted, depressed, and anxious, and craves even more of the drug to reverse this terrible feeling. After "crashing," an abuser may fall into a deep sleep that can last for days.

Get the Facts

All of the tragedies you read about at the beginning of this chapter might have been prevented if the people involved had asked for help with their drug problems or if their friends or family members had discovered the problem and been able to help. If you suspect that someone you know is abusing amphetamines, don't be afraid to tell your parents, guidance counselor, coach, or school nurse, or another adult you trust. Try not to feel bad about seeking help. After all, good friends care about their friends and want them to be healthy and safe. Getting help may be the best thing you can do for someone in trouble. In Chapter 5, we'll look at some of the ways you can tell whether a friend or family member has been abusing amphetamines or other drugs and how you may be able to help.

It's important that kids learn how risky drug use can be so that you can make your own decision to stay drug-free. By learning more about the dangers of amphetamines, you can take a big step toward protecting your health and that of your friends and family.

In September 1998, these children in Pacoima, California, got sick when one of their classmates brought a substance believed to be cocaine to the school and shared it with his friends. Some amphetamines and other stimulants were once used as diet aids, "pep pills," or stay-awake drugs, but today we know that using them illegally can be dangerous. One of the best ways to avoid being harmed by such drugs is to learn what they are and how they affect your mind and body.

A HISTORY OF AMPHETAMINES

Most amphetamines are **synthetic** drugs, which means that they are not grown in nature or extracted from plants. Rather, they are created in chemical facilities or illegally in makeshift laboratories.

Although amphetamine was first synthesized by a German scientist in 1887, it was forgotten until the early 1930s. At that time, scientists discovered that the drug could increase blood pressure and was useful in treating lung congestion. In 1932 an American **pharmaceutical** (medicinal) company called Smith, Klein & French began marketing a nasal inhaler containing amphetamine under the trade name Benzedrine. The drug relieved nasal congestion from colds, hay fever, and asthma. The company soon began selling a tablet form of Benzedrine as well.

Three years later, Smith, Klein & French discovered

the drug's stimulating effects, and amphetamine was reported effective in treating narcolepsy and Parkinson's disease (a disorder of the nervous system). Not long after, the American Medical Association approved the use of amphetamine for these disorders but added a warning that "continuous overdosage" might cause "restlessness and sleeplessness." Most physicians did not believe that the drug had any serious side effects, however. For the next 11 years, the public showed increased interest in the drug, which was still believed to be nonaddictive and without harmful side effects.

The list of accepted uses for amphetamine grew longer and eventually included treatment for tobacco smoking, low blood pressure, persistent hiccups, and morphine addiction. As different uses for amphetamine were proposed, additional forms of the drug were developed. They included dextroamphetamine, marketed under the brand name Dexedrine; and methamphetamine, marketed as Desoxyn and Methedrine.

The New Cure-All Drug

Amphetamines became so popular that during World War II they were regularly given to American soldiers as "pep pills" to counteract fatigue and increase endurance. Germany also prescribed amphetamines to its Panzer troops. During this period, both legal and illegal versions of amphetamines became common.

When American soldiers came home from the war with news of this drug, the demand for amphetamine increased among the U.S. civilian population. In other

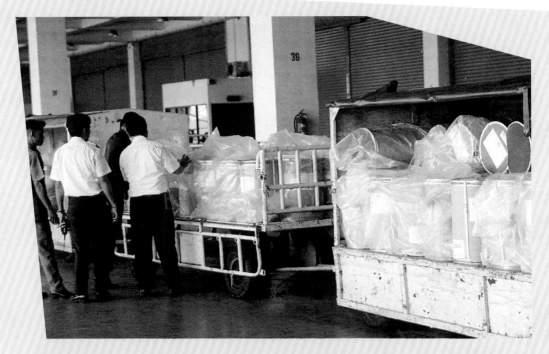

Police officers in Thailand inspect more than two tons of ephedrine that was seized in January 1998 while being smuggled from India to North Korea for use in making methamphetamine. One of the most addictive and deadly drugs known, methamphetamine, also called "ice" or "crystal meth," can affect a user's brain chemistry for up to six months after it is taken. It can also cause permanent brain damage.

parts of the world, especially Japan and Scandinavia, huge supplies of the drug that had been manufactured for soldiers were "dumped" on the civilian market. Pharmaceutical companies began to advertise them as a means of coping with the stresses of daily life.

The use of amphetamines—both in pill form and in a solution that could be injected—became so widespread that in 1954 in Japan, two million out of 88.5 million people were taking the drug. By then, however, people were beginning to learn about the dangers of amphetamine abuse. The Japanese government launched education and treatment programs and instituted penalties for selling or using the drug, and its use declined.

In the United States, amphetamines were still widely available as over-the-counter drugs. College students and truck drivers used them to stay awake for long periods of time. Housewives took the drug to curb their appetites and lose weight. Athletes took it as part of their physical training. Doctors prescribed amphetamines not only for weight loss but also in combination with other drugs to "cure" depression. American soldiers stationed in Korea and Japan began mixing speed with **heroin** to create a dangerous intravenous drug called a **speedball**. By the 1960s, even race horses were given amphetamines in the hope that the drug would increase their stamina and speed and help them win. (This practice ended in 1969, making horse racing the first American sport to adopt drug regulations.)

By 1965, an extensive **black market** (illegal production and sale) for the distribution of amphetamines had developed in the United States. Abuse of the drug was common. Methamphetamine was taken intravenously in huge doses by drug users known as "speed freaks." The problem was made worse by the fact that Methedrine was used in drug treatment programs as a cure for heroin addiction. Although Smith, Klein & French had discontinued the Benzedrine inhaler in 1949, other types of amphetamine inhalers were still being sold over the counter as cold remedies.

Controlling Amphetamine Use

Finally, the Food and Drug Administration, or FDA (a branch of government that regulates all food and medicine sold in the United States), took measures to decrease the amount of amphetamines in circulation. The FDA launched an anti-drug campaign in the early 1960s with the slogan "speed kills" to warn people about the dangers of amphetamine use. Many products that contained amphetamines were discontinued. Doctors prescribed amphetamines less frequently after they began observing the problems that their patients developed from using the drugs. In 1970, a law known as the **Controlled Substances Act** organized drugs into five categories, called schedules, that regulated their use in the United States. Amphetamines were listed as **Schedule II drugs**—those that have proven medical value but a high potential for abuse.

Unfortunately, the new regulations only increased the availability of amphetamines on the black market. Today, abuse of amphetamines continues, despite public awareness of its dangers. The worst amphetamine problem in the United States is with a powerful new form of methamphetamine known as "ice."

Types of Methamphetamine

Ice was originally smuggled into the United States from Hong Kong, Korea, and the Philippines in the 1980s. It became the number-one drug problem in Hawaii in the early 1990s, and its manufacture and abuse

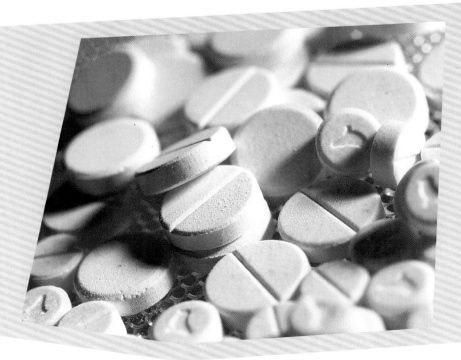

The drug known as Ecstasy may sound pleasant, but in reality it can be quite dangerous. It is manufactured from methamphetamine and a hallucinogen known as MDA.

quickly spread to California and other western states.

The drug earned its nickname from its appearance—it looks like clear chunks of frozen water. It is commonly smoked like crack cocaine, but its effects last much longer: a high can last from 8 to 24 hours. Ice can be made cheaply from a variety of chemical compounds. Some samples of crystal meth have had purity levels as high as 98 to 100 percent. A single gram can give the user 10 to 15 "hits" (doses) of the drug.

The most popular way of using methamphetamine is snorting (inhaling through the nose), but it is also smoked as ice, taken in pill form, or injected. Methamphetamine abuse has been associated with paranoia, strokes, and heart attacks. Like other amphetamines, it causes the user to become irritable, easily excitable, aggressive, hyperactive, and suspicious. Mood swings are common under the influence of methamphetamine. Withdrawal from high doses of this unpredictable and deadly drug produces severe depression. In long-term users, methamphetamine can cause permanent brain damage. In recent years, a dramatic increase in overdose deaths has also occurred.

Dr. Michael Abrams of Broadlawn Medical Center in Des Moines, Iowa, describes methamphetamine as "the most malignant addictive drug known to mankind." Dr. Alan Leshner, director of the National Institute on Drug Abuse, says that the drug can affect a user's brain chemistry for up to six months following binge use. Some people fear that because the drug is so addictive and is cheaper than cocaine, an **epidemic** (widespread outbreak) of methamphetamine use is possible.

Scientists are still studying this drug and what it does to the body, but at present there are no medications to combat the effects of methamphetamine abuse. The U.S. government has been funding research in this area.

Where Does Methamphetamine Come From?

The illegal sale and abuse of methamphetamine has become a growing problem in the United States, particularly in the western part of the country. At first, methamphetamine was primarily sold by outlaw gangs and other criminal groups. Now, large organized crime rings operating out of Mexico and specializing in illegal drugs—including marijuana, cocaine, and heroin—conduct most of the methamphetamine distribution in the United States. Such crime syndicates already have distribution markets in place from dealing in other drugs. These organizations buy large quantities of ephedrine, one of the ingredients for making methamphetamine, from other countries.

Methamphetamine and Violence

Sometimes drug users lose their jobs because of their habit. They may turn to crimes, such as burglary or armed robbery, to obtain money for drugs. "Meth" users also exhibit hostile behavior produced directly by the drug. Chronic use of meth can cause **paranoid psychosis**, a condition that includes **delusions** (persistent false beliefs) and hallucinations that may cause the user to attack others because of his or her paranoia. For instance, a heavy methamphetamine user may hear imaginary voices commanding him to injure other people.

Because methamphetamine produces extreme agitation, it is frequently implicated in cases of domestic violence, when a husband or wife attacks a spouse or their children. Police in Contra Costa County, California, report that methamphetamine is involved in nearly 90 percent of the family disputes investigated by that agency.

Ecstasy: a Hallucinogenic Stimulant

Ecstasy, or **MDMA** (3,4-methylenedioxymethamphetamine), is a synthetic stimulant, one that is not

found in nature. It is produced from two other dangerous drugs: methamphetamine and a mind-altering
substance known as **MDA** (3,4-methylenedioxyamphet-
amine). It has the effects of speed and also the effects of
hallucinogens (drugs that distort perception of objects
or events or that cause the user to perceive objects or
visions that are not real).

Ecstasy and other substances that are synthetically
produced and resemble prescription drugs are often
called **designer drugs**. The chemical structure of a
designer drug may differ from that of its parent drug by
only a few atoms. But until late 1986, the laws regulat-
ing drug research and production in the United States
allowed designer drugs to be produced and sold legally
because they were not identical to controlled drugs.

Ecstasy became popular in the 1980s, when a group
of psychotherapists discovered that it was useful in
treating patients during therapy sessions. But the effects
of the drug were difficult to control, so it was no longer
used as medication and it was quickly classified as a
Schedule I drug, meaning that it has a high potential
for abuse and has no known medical use. (Marijuana,
LSD, and heroin are other Schedule I drugs.)

Sold illegally, Ecstasy is sometimes called "Adam,"
"X," "XTC," "clarity," "essence," or "love drug." It is
usually swallowed in tablet, capsule, or powder form,
but it is also used intravenously. Sometimes Ecstasy is
combined with other drugs such as methadone, **fentanyl**, heroin and other **opiates**, LSD, or **ketamine** (an
animal tranquilizer that, when used by humans, has

hallucinogenic and painkilling properties).

Ecstasy is popular among college students and young professionals, especially those who participate in "raves" or all-night dance parties. Certain areas of the United States have higher uses of the drug; they include California, Texas, New York, Florida, and New England.

Herbal Ecstasy

Herbal drugs are substances derived from plant matter that usually appear in plant form rather than in capsules or pills. They are often marketed as safe and effective because they are "natural," but this is simply a way to convince people to buy them. And because they are usually sold as nutritional supplements rather than drugs, they are not regulated by the FDA. This means that the user cannot be certain of the quality or strength of these drugs.

Herbal Ecstasy is actually ephedrine, a stimulant whose effects can mimic some of the signs of MDMA intoxication. It is sold in pill form, as a loose herb, and as a preparation used to make a kind of tea that treats asthma. It is sometimes called "herbal bliss," "rave energy," "ritual spirit," "GWM," "herbal X," "ultimate Xphoria," or "X."

Although herbal Ecstasy is not classified as an illegal drug, it is a dangerous substance that can cause high blood pressure, strokes, heart attacks, and seizures. Such reactions are so common that the FDA is thinking about putting restrictions on the drug. More than 800 reports filed with government agencies describe the bad reactions

Some people believe that substances advertised as "natural" or "herbal" are safe to use. In reality, most of these drugs are not regulated and can be just as harmful as illegal stimulants like amphetamines.

users have experienced after taking herbal Ecstasy.

Who Uses Amphetamines?

Stimulants are among the most widely abused drugs in the United States, especially among teens and young adults. College students and young professionals who are involved in the "club scene" or who attend all-night raves frequently abuse these drugs. They also use other dangerous drugs, including LSD, marijuana, ketamine, and alcohol.

The Drug Abuse Warning Network (DAWN) is an organization that studies illegal drug use and helps to

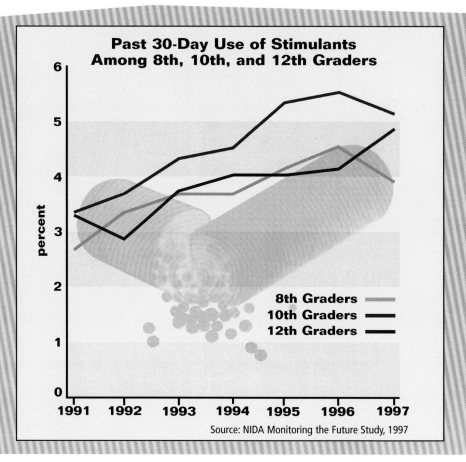

Past 30-Day Use of Stimulants Among 8th, 10th, and 12th Graders

8th Graders ——
10th Graders ——
12th Graders ——

Source: NIDA Monitoring the Future Study, 1997

This graph shows the results of a yearly survey by the National Institute on Drug Abuse in which eighth, tenth, and twelfth graders were asked whether they had used stimulants in the 30 days before each survey was taken. Although stimulant abuse is low among all grades—less than 6 percent of kids use these drugs—it appears to be highest among tenth graders, and it is on the rise among twelfth graders.

predict future trends in drug abuse. DAWN publishes surveys of the number of people who arrive in hospital emergency rooms after taking illegal drugs, and it also gathers information from medical examiners—doctors who conduct autopsies to determine causes of death.

DAWN documented that most of the people who died while taking amphetamines between 1991 and 1994 were white males aged 25 to 39. It also reported that emergency room episodes involving methamphetamine have increased steadily since 1992. Although amphetamine abuse is a problem across the United States, the hardest hit areas are in the West.

Amphetamines and the Law

One of the problems with controlling amphetamine abuse has been that the ingredients used to create many of these stimulants are not illegal. In 1996, the U.S. government passed a law called the Comprehensive Methamphetamine Control Act that strictly regulates the sale of large quantities of the chemicals used to produce that drug. It also increased penalties for trafficking (selling illegally) and for producing or possessing equipment that is used in manufacturing controlled substances. The Methamphetamine Control Act also provided funds for research and public monitoring of drug use and launched education programs to inform the public about this dangerous drug.

Why are amphetamines so strictly regulated? What makes them dangerous, even deadly? We'll learn the answers to these questions in Chapter 3.

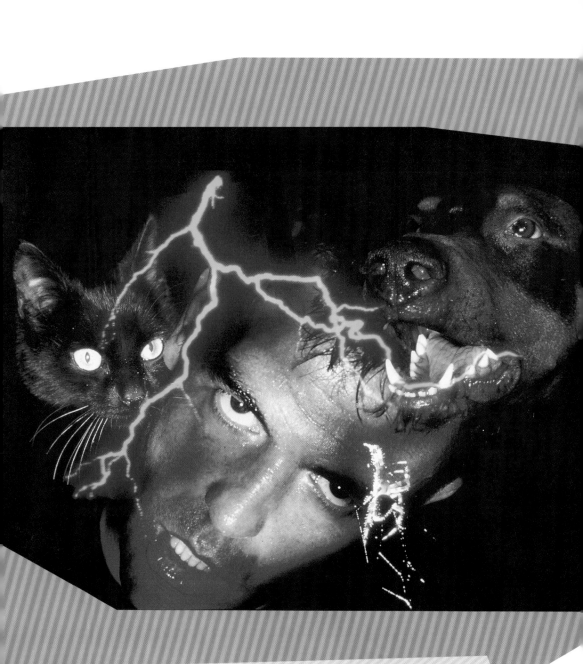

The effects of amphetamines and other stimulants on your brain can be frightening. Users of these drugs may feel paranoia (persistent irrational fears) and anxiety. They may also experience nightmarish hallucinations.

WHAT STIMULANTS DO TO YOUR BRAIN AND BODY

In many ways, the brain is the most fascinating and important organ in the body. The brain determines your personality—who you are and what you think, feel, and do. The brain allows people to build skyscrapers, write symphonies, solve algebraic equations, invent airplanes, speak languages, feel love and hate, dream up new ideas, make decisions, and read books. At the same time, the brain regulates unconscious activity in the body, such as your heart rate, digestion, and breathing.

This complicated and wonderful organ is the headquarters of your body's command and control center, called the nervous system. Elongated nerve cells known as **neurons**, located in the brain and spinal cord, send out and receive messages that govern everything you do. They are grouped in specific patterns and locations to act

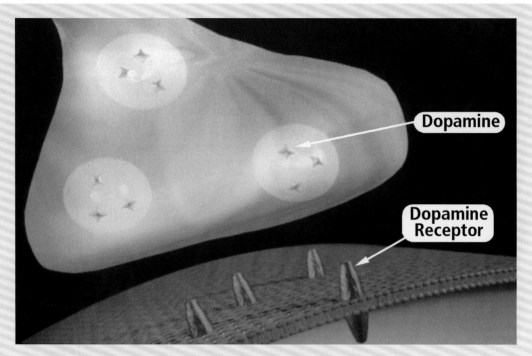

These drawings show close-up views of a synapse (the space between nerve endings) in the brain. Normally, after neurotransmitters such as dopamine (shown in orange) are released, they attach themselves to special receptor sites on the neuron. Drugs such as cocaine

as relay stations for the various activities of your body. The human brain contains about 100 billion neurons.

Neurons are connected by **axons** along which electrical impulses send messages between your brain and your body. When the message reaches the end of an axon, it is sent chemically to the next neuron, where it is received by structures called **dendrites**. This process happens within fractions of a second. It allows messages to pass between one part of your brain and another, and between your brain and the rest of your body.

(shown in green above) attach to the same receptor sites and block the absorption of dopamine. As a result, dopamine builds up in the synapse and produces a brief feeling of euphoria or a "high."

Neurons send messages to each other by releasing special chemicals called **neurotransmitters**. These chemicals work by attaching themselves to key sites on neurons called **receptor sites**. About 30 different types of neurotransmitters have been discovered in the human brain. The ones that are most affected by amphetamines are **norepinephrine** and **dopamine**. Cocaine also affects the dopamine neurotransmitter. Some stimulants, such as Ecstasy, affect another neuro-transmitter called **serotonin**.

What Amphetamines Do to Your Brain

Amphetamines change the way the brain works by changing the way neurons communicate. Normally, once a neurotransmitter has attached to a neuron's receptor site and caused a change in the cell, it is pumped back to the neuron that released it. But a stimulant, such as cocaine, blocks the pump and causes the neurotransmitter to build up in the gap (or **synapse**) between neurons. As a result, the chemical keeps affecting neurons long after it should have stopped.

Each type of neurotransmitter affects the brain differently. For example, dopamine is released by neurons in the **limbic system**—the part of the brain that controls feelings of pleasure. Norepinephrine does a very different job: it prepares the body and mind for an emergency by making the heart beat faster and expanding the breathing tubes to make breathing easier. This is often called a "fight-or-flight" response, because it prepares your body to react to a stressful situation either by fighting (staying put) or by running away (escaping).

Amphetamines cause both dopamine and norepinephrine to build up in the brain, so while dopamine produces feelings of pleasure for a short time, norepinephrine increases heart rate, blood pressure, and pulse rate. This may explain why amphetamines were originally prescribed for weight loss—the body does not need food when swift action and decision-making are more necessary for survival.

What Amphetamines Do to Your Body

A drug that is swallowed must first pass through the liver, which detoxifies it, or breaks it down into **nontoxic** (not poisonous) substances. Through this process, the liver protects the body from some poisons. When amphetamines or any drug are smoked or injected, however, they go directly to the brain from the lungs or veins. They are much stronger by the time they reach the brain, since they haven't been broken down by the body.

Once a drug is in the bloodstream, it is absorbed by tissues it encounters. The higher the concentration of the drug in a certain region of the body, the more damage occurs there. For this reason, parts of the body with many blood vessels, such as the lungs, brain, heart, and kidneys, are more likely to be damaged from drug abuse.

As we have seen, amphetamines not only increase blood pressure and heart rate but can also cause irregular heartbeats. Very high doses may cause permanent damage to blood vessels in the brain. Amphetamines also cause dry mouth and dilated (widened) pupils. Dilated pupils make users extremely sensitive to light, so they may wear sunglasses even at night. Users may also have blurred vision for the same reason.

Amphetamines increase breathing rate and the rate at which the body uses its stored energy. Long-term users of amphetamines can lose up to 20 percent of their normal body weight. Other physical effects include headaches, nausea, vomiting, increased blood sugar, and excessive salivation.

(continued on p. 44)

Amphetamine Use and AIDS

t's a proven fact: if you use drugs intravenously (inject them into a vein), you run a high risk of becoming infected with the human immunodeficiency virus (HIV)—the virus that causes AIDS.

AIDS (acquired immunodeficiency syndrome) is caused when HIV has infected the body and diminished its natural immunity to disease. People who have AIDS are vulnerable to illnesses that rarely affect a person with a healthy immune system.

AIDS is often fatal. Before 1996, when new drug treatments were developed, contracting AIDS was considered a death sentence. Until that year, 85 to 90 percent of all AIDS patients died within three years. But the news in 1996 wasn't all good. That same year, a White House study reported that one in four new HIV infections occurred among young people aged 13 to 20.

Intravenous (or IV) drug users are the second-largest group at risk for contracting HIV. They make up about 25 to 30 percent of the total number of current AIDS cases. HIV cannot be passed by casual contact, such as shaking hands, hugging, or kissing on the cheek or on the lips; it can only be passed through infected blood, through sexual contact with an infected person, or from an infected mother to her baby. The disease is common among IV drug users because addicts often share their hypodermic needles when "shooting up." Injecting leaves a tiny amount of blood on the needle—enough to transmit HIV to a person who uses the same needle as someone who has the virus.

HIV can also be passed from an infected IV drug user to his or her sexual partners if the people involved practice unprotected sex (sex without a latex condom). Amphetamines and other drugs can also decrease users' inhibitions, leading them to do things they normally wouldn't do while "sober," such as engaging in unsafe sex.

The best way to protect yourself from HIV and AIDS is to avoid intravenous drug use and to abstain from sexual contact. If someone asks you to try injecting cocaine or other amphetamines, just ask yourself: is this worth dying for?

This chart shows the number of AIDS cases in the United States by "exposure category," meaning the way in which each person contracted HIV. Intravenous drug users make up the second-largest group of people who currently suffer from AIDS.

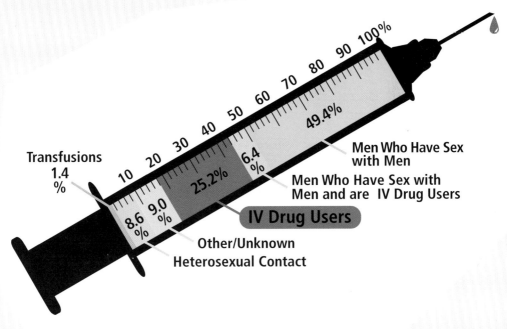

Source: Centers for Disease Control, 1996

(continued from p. 41)

What Ecstasy Does to Your Brain and Body

Ecstasy acts in a similar way to other amphetamines. It remains in the body for at least three hours, and its effects can last up to 24 hours. Scientists aren't sure what kind of long-term damage Ecstasy does to the brain, but they know that it affects the neurotransmitter known as serotonin, which affects mood and personality.

Ecstasy produces a sense of euphoria or well-being, but it can also cause anxiety and paranoia. Heavy doses may give the user the sensation of floating. As with other amphetamines, Ecstasy users can become depressed, violent, or **irrational**, or may experience hallucinations. Side effects include loss of appetite, nausea, vomiting, blurred vision, chills, faintness, sweating, tremors, increased blood pressure and heart rate, insomnia, loss of control over body movements, and convulsions. Some of these effects can last for weeks after taking the drug. Because Ecstasy also causes a great increase in body temperature, it may be responsible for muscle breakdown and kidney failure. For this reason, when it is used during strenuous activities such as dancing or in hot weather, Ecstasy can cause fatal **dehydration** (loss of water and body fluids).

Injecting Amphetamines

When people who inject amphetamines or other drugs share hypodermic needles, they run the risk of contracting **HIV**, or human immunodeficiency virus, from another user. (Read the article in this chapter about

Did you know that a mother who abuses drugs while she is pregnant can cause her child to be born addicted? This is because nutrients are passed through the mother's bloodstream to the fetus by way of the umbilical cord. Any chemicals or drugs the mother takes can be passed to the fetus. The women shown here gave birth to crack-addicted babies, but have joined a New York drug treatment program that has helped them and their children become drug-free.

the danger of becoming infected with HIV when injecting amphetamines.) HIV is spread through infected blood or sexual contact with an infected person. It is the virus that causes **AIDS** (acquired immunodeficiency syndrome), for which there is no known cure. Sharing needles can also transmit other diseases and infections, such as **hepatitis** (inflammation of the liver) and **endo-carditis** (inflammation of the heart lining and valves).

A common problem among intravenous drug users is damage to the veins. Injecting regularly can cause veins to collapse and infections to develop around the area of the collapsed vein. Addicts who are not careful or skilled in injecting can also kill themselves by accidentally inject-ing air into a vein. An air bubble in the bloodstream can reach the brain within a few seconds and cause death.

Another danger stems from the fact that the quality and purity of illegal amphetamines are not controlled or regulated. A user's supply may be diluted, or "cut," so that the drug dealer can earn more money by stretching the supply. Sugar, caffeine, flour, and talcum powder are common substances added to amphetamines. Sometimes the drug is also cut with other drugs, which increases the possibility of an overdose. And if additives do not dissolve properly, they can clog blood vessels leading to the lungs, liver, kidneys, or brain and cause serious infections in those organs.

Stimulants and Pregnancy

Amphetamines taken by pregnant women pose a great risk to their unborn children. The embryo (group of cells that will become an infant) is most vulnerable to these drugs: the liver is not developed enough to detoxify such substances, and since the fetus is so small, an amphetamine dose taken by the adult mother is an overdose for the child and may cause permanent damage or death.

One study of mothers who took amphetamines during pregnancy indicates that premature births were 25 percent more common among the drug users. And among those who used amphetamines throughout their pregnancy, the rate of infant death occurring just before or in the first month after birth was 7.5 percent higher than the infant death rate among women who stopped taking amphetamines early in pregnancy. Babies of mothers who continually used amphetamines during pregnancy also had more physical abnormalities and social problems. In the same study, one third of the children born to amphetamine users later had to be put in foster homes away from their drug-using mothers.

Now that you know what amphetamines and other stimulants can do, you may wonder why anyone would risk their lives by taking such drugs. In the next two chapters, we'll examine some of the reasons people use drugs and how you can avoid using them yourself.

Do you smoke cigarettes because most of your friends do? Do you drink beer because it makes you feel "mellow"? Do you use marijuana or speed because you know your parents disapprove? Guess what? You're not alone. These reasons reflect perfectly normal emotions. Yet there are many drug-free ways to fit in, relax, or communicate with your parents. Read the next two chapters for some ideas.

WHY DO PEOPLE USE AMPHETAMINES?

W hen youngsters reach adolescence, they begin the sometimes-difficult transition from childhood to adulthood. Erik Erikson, the author of a famous book on childhood and society called *Insight and Responsibility*, wrote that one's teen years are a time of feeling uprooted. "Like a trapeze artist, the young person in the middle of vigorous motion must let go of his safe hold on childhood and reach out for a firm grasp on adulthood," Erikson wrote.

Some adolescents don't feel as close to their parents or siblings as they once did. You might feel like friends understand you better because they're going through the same kinds of changes. And while you're trying to figure out exactly who you are, your body has also begun to change or will very soon. These upheavals may make you feel insecure, angry, or frightened. You may find that you want to rebel against your parents and other grown-ups who have authority, such as teachers and religious leaders. Some kids who feel this way mistakenly believe that using drugs and engaging in other types of risky behavior are acts of independence that can make them feel better about themselves.

If you think about why you experience certain emotions, you will realize that using drugs is not the answer to your problems. Rejecting healthy practices, safety, and common sense just because grown-ups tell you they are important will not help you. Making an unwise choice, such as using amphetamines, shows that the drug user is still a child who needs to be protected by adults.

Peer Pressure

We all know what it feels like to want to belong to a social group. No one wants to feel disliked or left out when a friend is having a party or a group of kids is hanging out. But what happens when someone in the group does something you don't agree with or don't want to do? You want to fit in; you want people to think you're cool.

This feeling is called **peer pressure**. Sometimes it's easy to spot: a friend might come right out and say something to make you feel bad if you don't do what everyone else seems to be doing. Other times, your friends might not say anything specific, but you still worry that they won't like you if you don't go along with them.

Peer pressure is one of the main reasons kids begin using drugs. Even adults feel peer pressure, but when you're still growing up and trying to figure out exactly where you fit in, that pressure can be much stronger.

If anyone asks you to try a chemical or unusual substance, tell them you're not interested in experimenting with chemicals that can hurt you.

"Instant" Society

Our society moves a lot faster than it used to. We can contact someone on the other side of the world instantly by using a telephone, fax machine, or Internet connection. Appliances such as microwave ovens help speed up processes that once took much longer. Advances in science and medicine help prevent and cure numerous illnesses that were once fatal and can shorten the time needed to recover from sickness or accidents.

These improvements have made life easier and better for millions of people. But they have also had another effect: because everything seems to be moving and working so quickly, some people expect instant solutions to all of their problems.

Many important parts of life—learning, being creative, growing physically, and accomplishing great things—take time and energy. Overcoming serious difficulties also requires endurance and concentration. Some people become easily frustrated when their desires are not met or problems cannot be solved right away. A few decide that taking chemicals into their bodies will bring instant happiness, pleasure, or insight. Instead, they get misery, discomfort, more problems, and sometimes addiction.

(continued on p. 54)

Ten Dumb Reasons To Do Drugs

1 **You're bored.** Anything easy gets boring after a while. Drinking and using other drugs will get boring, too, but by the time they do, you may have a hard time stopping. Find pleasure in the many alternatives available to you. Real life—without drugs—is anything but dull.

2 **You want to feel grown up.** Doing drugs is actually a way to avoid the responsibilities of adulthood. If you start drinking or using other drugs at age 13, you will stay 13 emotionally until you quit. Adults who abuse alcohol or other drugs are acting childish. Don't copy them.

3 **You want to forget your problems.** Your problems won't go away when you're high or drunk. They may even get worse. And you can develop a problem that's even greater than the ones you're trying to forget: addiction.

4 **You want to be accepted.** Friendships based on getting drunk or high can quickly get boring. You end up doing the same old thing over and over. Such friendships fail to grow. Sometimes they aren't even real, because if you do refuse alcohol or drugs, many of these "friends" will no longer want to spend time with you. True friendship is based on mutual interests and on respect. Drugs keep friends from building trust, staying committed to the friendship, and communicating honestly with one another.

5 **You don't want to put down your friends who drink or do other drugs.** If these people really are your friends, a simple "no, thanks" won't seem like an insult to them. There are ways to excuse yourself from taking drugs without criticizing anyone or hurting their feelings.

6 **You want to see how it feels to be drunk or high.** Too many kids try alcohol or other drugs for this very reason and end up in Alcoholics Anonymous or strung out on heroin. You might also want to try driving a race car, sky diving, or flying a plane, but you need to wait until you are old enough and are adequately prepared and supervised. By the time you are older, you may not want to try any of these dangerous activities.

7 **It feels good to get drunk or high.** Usually it doesn't feel so great the first time you down a beer, take speed, or smoke a joint. In fact, you may feel horrible the first time and every time after. But this may not stop you from using or overdosing on drugs. Becoming addicted means that you continue to use drugs despite how bad you feel or how they're messing up your life.

8 **Everybody is doing drugs.** Not true. But even if it were, it's a dumb reason for you to do something. What about using your own mind and heart to decide what you really want to do, what is best for you and not someone else?

9 **Your parents get drunk or do other drugs.** This is not a good situation in which to grow up. It can be confusing and painful. But instead of making the same mistakes your parents may be making, you can choose to lead a different life. You might want to seek counseling for the support and encouragement that you have trouble finding at home. Maybe your parents will even go with you to a family counselor.

10 **Your parents don't care about you.** If this is true, you certainly could bury your sadness under gallons of wine coolers and mounds of cocaine. But this will not change your situation, and it will add one more person to the list of people who are uncaring: you. Seek counseling instead. You need to learn how to care about yourself and find others who are able to care about you. Perhaps your parents will surprise you and show that they actually do care by attending counseling with you.

(continued from p.51)

Mixed Messages

Companies eager to sell their products often use words or images in their advertising to suggest that these items will provide instant gratification (meaning reward or pleasure). If you use this toothpaste, wear this clothing, or drive this car, the ads seem to say, you will be successful, beautiful, popular, and happy.

Some of the models used to advertise products in recent years have been made to look as though they are sick from using drugs. For example, the so-called "heroin chic" style of modeling features pale, underweight young men and women with dark circles under their eyes, dressed in torn or scanty clothing. Seeing these models on billboards, in magazines, and on television may give some teens the idea that heroin and other drugs are glamorous or cool.

But when you think about it, this is actually a different kind of peer pressure. Advertisers count on your looking at these images and seeing the models as kids like you—and wanting to buy the company's products to fit in. If celebrities and models are using drugs, the ads seem to say, why not you?

You know why. Taking drugs is foolish. It endangers your life. It can destroy your health, your family, and your grades. It is important to remember that *most kids don't take drugs of any kind*. The great majority of young people never abuse amphetamines or other drugs. If TV shows, movies, magazine ads, radio programs, video games, music, or Internet sites try to idealize drugs, they

Despite what you may see and hear on the Internet, in the lyrics of popular songs, and on television, drugs cannot provide quick solutions to your problems. In fact, most kids discover that using drugs actually creates even bigger problems.

are doing so in the hope of selling you something.

Use your common sense. Don't sell yourself short by falling for such material. Drugs can never magically provide excitement, sex appeal, ecstasy, or enlightenment any more than the other products advertisers want you to buy.

What if you or your friends have already tried drugs? Is it too late to stop? How can you help someone else who is caught up in drug abuse? Chapter 5 will help you find some answers to these questions.

Missouri Governor Mel Carnahan announces the state's "life or meth" anti-drug campaign during a news conference in March 1998. The poster of a burning teenager on the governor's right is one of three that were distributed to schools to make students aware of the dangers of producing and using methamphetamines. Does your state or local government have a similar program?

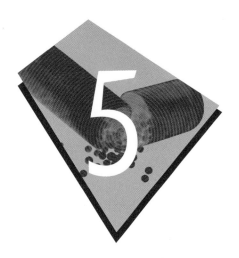

GETTING HELP

Discovering whether a friend or loved one has a problem with amphetamines—or with any other drug, including alcohol, tobacco, or marijuana—isn't always easy. Children as young as fourth-graders sometimes begin experimenting with alcohol or other drugs. Many amphetamine abusers are **polydrug users**, which means that they use many drugs depending on what is available.

How Can I Tell If Someone I Know Has a Drug Problem?

Most people who are having difficulties with drugs will not simply go to a close friend and ask for help. In fact, drug abusers are more likely to deny the problem and try to hide the symptoms. They may be embarrassed or afraid to confide in someone else. Still, there are some warning signs that you can look for if you suspect that a friend or loved one is abusing alcohol or other drugs. If someone you know displays one or more of the following traits, he or she may have a drug problem:

- Getting high or getting drunk on a regular basis
- Lying about the amount of alcohol or other drugs being used
- Avoiding you or other friends to get high or drunk
- Giving up activities such as sports, homework, or hanging out with friends who don't drink alcohol or use other drugs
- Having to drink more alcohol or use increasing amounts of another drug to get the same effect
- Constantly talking about drinking alcohol or using other drugs
- Pressuring other people to drink alcohol or use other drugs
- Believing that alcohol or other drugs are needed to have fun
- Getting into trouble with the law or getting suspended from school for an alcohol- or other drug-related incident
- Taking risks, including sexual risks or driving under the influence of alcohol or other drugs
- Feeling tired, run-down, hopeless, depressed, or even suicidal
- Missing work or school, or performing tasks poorly because of alcohol or other drug use

Keep in mind that some of these signs, such as mood

How to Tell If *You* Have a Drug Problem

Drug and alcohol problems affect all kinds of people, regardless of age, sex, race, income level, or way of life. If you abuse drugs or alcohol and think you're not like others who do, you're wrong. Just like anyone else who abuses drugs, you can seriously endanger your body and mind—and even your life. To find out whether you have a problem, try to answer the following questions honestly:

- Can I predict the next time I will use drugs or get drunk?
- Do I think that I need alcohol or other drugs to have fun?
- Do I turn to alcohol or other drugs to make myself feel better after an argument or confrontation?
- Do I have to drink more or use more drugs to get the same effect I once felt with a smaller amount?
- Do I drink alcohol or use other drugs when I'm alone?
- When I drink alcohol or use other drugs, do I forget certain segments of time?
- Am I having trouble at work or school because of alcohol or other drug use?
- Do I make promises to others or to myself to stop drinking alcohol or using other drugs, but then break them?
- Do I feel alone, scared, miserable, or depressed?

If you answered "yes" to any of the above questions, you may have a drug problem. Don't be discouraged, though. You are not alone. Millions of people around the world have triumphed over drug abuse and are now living healthy, drug-free lives.

changes, poor job or school performance, and depression, might be signs of other problems. They could also be symptoms of an illness that you may not know about. Nevertheless, these danger signs indicate that something is wrong.

Be sure to talk to an adult you trust or one who is trained to recognize abuse of alcohol and other drugs. A parent or other adult family member, or a doctor, nurse, religious leader, school counselor, or coach can give you advice about what to do next. This is not being disloyal! You don't even have to mention the person's name. But talking to a professional will help you figure out what you can do to help.

What Are the Signs That Someone Is Using Amphetamines?

A person who often uses amphetamines develops physical, mental, and behavioral signs of having been poisoned. Frequently, abusers look sickly and begin to neglect themselves. They may wash less frequently or neglect their clothing or appearance. If the abuser has been injecting amphetamines, you may also see needle marks on the arms or other parts of the body.

An amphetamine abuser is often extremely restless, nervous, anxious, or worried. He or she may talk constantly or speak very quickly. A person using "speed" will often pace or show other forms of **compulsion** (behavior that is very difficult to control), such as repeating an action or task over and over. To raise money for purchasing drugs, users may sell clothing,

Like other hallucinogens, amphetamines can cause users to see, hear, and feel things in a distorted way. With amphetamine abuse, however, the user is often unaware that the drug is producing these illusions and distortions.

jewelry, household items, or other possessions.

Amphetamine abusers' eyes become more sensitive to light, so they might wear sunglasses constantly. When a user has binged on amphetamines, he or she may go without sleep for extremely long periods of time and then sleep for days. After the effects of the drug wear off, a user often feels deeply depressed and in some cases may even attempt suicide.

Stimulant abusers can also become easily enraged or even violent, sometimes directing their anger at inanimate (not living) objects such as furniture or

Boxing great Sugar Ray Leonard gives sparring lessons to fifth graders at Sierra Vista Elementary School in California. Leonard is among the many celebrities working with organizations such as D.A.R.E. America to inform kids about the dangers of illegal drugs. You can help, too: check out anti-drug programs at your school, library, or local community center. Learning about drugs is the best way to stay drug-free and healthy.

walls. Some abusers develop a mental illness called **amphetamine psychosis**. A person suffering from this condition may feel great fear and paranoia. He or she may also have visual, **auditory** (hearing), and **tactile** (touch) hallucinations. In other words, the drug user sees, hears, and feels things in a distorted way or perceives things that are not real. Although this also occurs when other hallucinogenic drugs are taken, the amphetamine user is not aware that the drug is producing these illusions and distortions.

An amphetamine user may experience the following effects after taking a dose:

- severe headaches
- heavy perspiring
- dry mouth
- dilated (enlarged) pupils
- tremors in the hands or fingers
- dizziness
- rapid breathing
- increased heart rate
- increased body temperature
- convulsions
- unconsciousness

A person who abuses amphetamines over a long period of time may show these signs:

- extreme weight loss
- pale skin
- odor of glue or mayonnaise
- decaying or discolored teeth
- scars or scabs from "crank bugs"

After an amphetamine binge, users experience a period sometimes known as "tweaking," when they can endanger themselves or others. In this stage, an amphetamine abuser's eyes may shift rapidly from side to side or jerk back and forth involuntarily. Tweakers may become excessively irritable, unpredictable, or even violent.

How Can I Help Someone Who Is High on Amphetamines?

Drug abuse specialists help tweakers recover from a drug binge by putting them in a place with very little stimulation—a darkened, quiet room, for example—and then calling for medical or police assistance. In severe cases, a doctor may even sedate the drug abuser to calm him or her.

Police officers are instructed to keep a safe distance from people who may be under the influence of amphetamines. They are told not to shine bright lights and to speak slowly and lower the pitch of their voices, since tweakers hear sounds at a fast pace and high pitch. Some stimulants also cause users to hear a constant, imaginary buzzing sound.

Another way to calm a person who is high on amphetamines is to move slowly, so that he or she won't misinterpret your actions as an attack and try to retaliate. For the same reason, you should keep your hands visible. Try to keep an amphetamine user talking, to avoid having them slip into delusional thinking. Any amphetamine user who appears to be in great distress or is unconscious should be taken to a hospital emergency room immediately.

If you discover that a friend or family member is using "speed," you should seek professional help for that person. Although no known drug can combat the effects of amphetamines, doctors can give amphetamine users medication to help the body eliminate the drug more

What Makes You Feel Better About Yourself?

In May 1998, *USA Weekend Magazine* conducted a survey of more than 250,000 students in grades 6 to 12 to find out what they thought of themselves and what most influenced their self-image. The survey asked kids what they liked most and least about themselves. Half of the students said they felt "really good" about themselves, and half said they did not. The chart below shows the number of teens who chose ways they thought they could improve themselves and enhance their self-image:

Question: Which of the following would make you feel better about yourself?*	
Getting better grades	49%
Bulking/toning up	38%
Losing weight	38%
Doing better at sports	36%
Better relationship with parents	30%
Wearing better clothes	24%
Fitting in with a certain crowd	16%
Nothing; I like myself the way I am	15%
Quitting smoking	8%

(*Teens responded to more than one choice in survey)

None of the students mentioned using drugs as a way to improve themselves. Using drugs will *not* help you to look better, feel better, or lead a more interesting life. But you can choose other ways to do so.

Source: *USA Weekend Magazine*, May 1, 1998

quickly. A drug treatment counselor can help the abuser identify the problems that may have led to drug use in the first place.

Where Do I Go for Help?

No matter where you live, you can find help for drug problems from numerous organizations, treatment centers, referral centers, and hotlines throughout the United States and Canada. There are different kinds of treatment services and centers. Some require their patients to remain at the center as **inpatients** for several weeks. Others provide **outpatient** counseling, meaning that patients attend scheduled therapy sessions but are free to return home after each treatment.

Various resources are listed in the back of this book. Some of the resources you may find in your community are:

- Drug hotlines
- Treatment centers
- City or local health departments
- Local branches of Alcoholics Anonymous, Al-Anon/Alateen, or Narcotics Anonymous
- Hospitals or emergency health clinics

Maybe you are hesitant or fearful about seeking help for yourself or someone you know. It may comfort you to know that most drug treatment programs are designed to provide group (or family) therapy for people with alcohol or drug problems, so no one has to face these troubles alone if they don't want to. All you have to do is pick up the phone and take the first step. The trained and experienced people on the other end of the line will take it from there.

Some people go through treatment a number of times before they recover completely. Don't give up if you or your loved one is not successful right away. Try to keep this in mind: research shows that when a drug abuser gets appropriate treatment—and when he or she follows the prescribed program—*treatment can work.* Getting treatment not only helps users conquer their drug problems but also gives them the skills and strength to conquer other challenges in the future.

GLOSSARY

addiction—a condition of some drug users that is caused by repeated drug use. An addict becomes physically dependent on the drug and continues to take it, despite severe negative consequences. Obtaining and using the drug take over the person's life. Amphetamines are highly addictive.

AIDS—acquired immunodeficiency syndrome; a defect of the immune system caused by the human immunodeficiency virus (HIV). AIDS is spread by the exchange of blood and by sexual contact; intravenous drug users have an increased risk of contracting HIV and developing AIDS.

amphetamine—an addictive stimulant, or a class of stimulants that includes this chemical.

amphetamine psychosis—a major mental disorder, characterized by derangement of the personality and loss of contact with reality, that is caused by amphetamine abuse.

auditory—related to hearing or sound.

axon—a long connector on a neuron that transmits messages from the neuron to other parts of the body.

binge—indulge excessively over a brief period of time.

black market—illegal production, distribution, or sale of a product or substance.

caffeine—a mild stimulant found in coffee, tea, chocolate, and some cola drinks and over-the-counter medicines.

cardiovascular—involving or related to the heart and blood vessels.

chronic—lasting over a long period of time or recurring frequently.

compulsion—an urge that is very hard to control.

Controlled Substances Act—a law passed in 1970 that organized drugs into five categories, called Schedules, that regulate their use in the United States.

dehydration—extreme loss of water from the body.

delusion—a persistent false belief.

dendrite—a branch-like structure on a neuron that receives messages from other parts of the body.

designer drug—a synthetic drug produced by chemically altering the structure of an original (often illegal) drug, or a drug that has been redesigned to increase appeal. Crack is a redesigned form of cocaine.

dextroamphetamine—a type of amphetamine sold under the brand name Dexedrine.

dopamine—a neurotransmitter in the brain. Dopamine is released by neurons in the limbic system, a part of the brain that controls feelings of pleasure.

Ecstasy—a combination of a hallucinogen called MDA and the stimulant methamphetamine. *See also MDMA.*

endocarditis—inflammation of the lining of the heart and its valves.

epidemic—an outbreak of a disease that spreads widely and rapidly.

euphoria—an intense feeling of happiness or well-being.

fentanyl—a synthetic drug with effects similar to those of the opiate morphine but much more potent.

hallucination—a distorted perception of objects or events, or an object or vision that is not real but is perceived by a person who has a mental disorder or who is using certain drugs.

hallucinogen—a substance that distorts the user's perception of objects or events or causes the user to perceive objects or visions that are not real.

hepatitis—inflammation of the liver.

heroin—the trade name given to diacetylmorphine, one of the strongest of the opiate drugs. Heroin is highly addictive.

HIV—human immunodeficiency virus, the virus that causes AIDS.

hyperactivity—a condition of being excessively or abnormally active.

inpatient—a patient who stays at, or is checked into, the clinic or hospital where treatment takes place.

insomnia—a chronic inability to sleep.

intravenous—introduced into the body through a vein.

irrational—not reasonable.

ketamine—also called "special K," an animal tranquilizer that when used by humans has hallucinogenic and painkilling properties.

limbic system—the region of the brain that controls emotions and feelings of pleasure.

MDA—3,4-methylenedioxyamphetamine, a hallucinogen used to make Ecstasy.

MDMA—3,4-methylenedioxymethamphetamine, also known as Ecstasy; a combination of a hallucinogen called MDA and the stimulant methamphetamine.

methamphetamine—a powerful form of amphetamine that is legally available by prescription under the name Desoxyn but is also illegally manufactured in different forms under various names, including "crank" and "ice."

neuron—nerve cell.

neurotransmitter—a chemical that is released by neurons and carries messages between them.

nicotine—a drug that occurs naturally in tobacco leaves and has both stimulant and depressant effects on the body. Nicotine is the addictive ingredient in tobacco.

nontoxic—not poisonous.

norepinephrine—a neurotransmitter in the brain. Norepinephrine helps to prepare the mind and body for emergencies by widening breathing tubes and making the heart beat faster.

opiate—any compound made from the milky juice of the poppy plant called *Papaver somniferum*, including opium, morphine, codeine, and heroin.

outpatient—a patient who visits a hospital, clinic, or other facility for treatment but is not required to check in.

paranoia—extreme, irrational distrust of others, accompanied by exaggerated fears.

paranoid psychosis—a major mental disorder characterized by derangement of the personality and loss of contact with reality. Patients also experience delusions and hallucinations, and feel extreme and unreasonable distrust and fear of others.

peer pressure—words or actions by a friend, a sibling, or someone else of your own age group that make you feel as though you have to act like them to fit in.

pharmaceutical—of or having to do with a pharmacy (a place where medicines are sold) or pharmacists (people trained in preparing drugs).

polydrug user—a person who uses a number of different drugs. Most stimulant abusers are polydrug users.

psychosis—a major mental disorder characterized by derangement of the personality and loss of contact with reality. Patients suffering from psychosis also experience delusions and hallucinations.

receptor site—a special area of a cell that combines with a chemical substance to alter the cell's function.

Schedule I drug—a substance that is considered unsafe to use, has no known medical value, and has a high potential for abuse. Marijuana, LSD, heroin, and Ecstasy are Schedule I drugs.

Schedule II drug—a substance that has a high potential for abuse but has proven medical value. Morphine, amphetamines, and codeine are Schedule II drugs.

serotonin—a neurotransmitter involved in the control of mood, aggression, and sexual behavior.

speedball—an injected mixture of "speed" (usually cocaine) and heroin.

stimulant—a drug that increases the body's activity.

synapse—a gap between neurons by which neurotransmitters carry messages.

synthetic—made by people rather than found in nature. Many amphetamines are synthetic drugs.

tactile—relating to the sense of touch.

tolerance—a condition in which a drug user needs increasing amounts of the drug to achieve the same level of intoxication obtained from using smaller amounts.

toxic—poisonous.

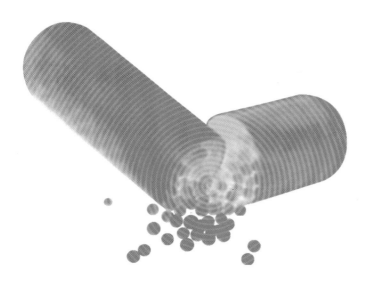

BIBLIOGRAPHY

Hazelden Publishing. *Methamphetamines*. 30 min. Hazelden Publishing, 1998. Videocassette.

Kaminski, Andrea. *Amphetamines*. Madison, WI: Wisconsin Clearinghouse, 1998.

____. *Methamphetamines*. Madison, WI: Wisconsin Clearing-house, 1998.

Lukas, Scott E. *Amphetamines: Danger in the Fast Lane*. New York: Chelsea House Publishers, 1992.

Morris, Brock, and Kevin Scheel. *Amphetamines*. 30 min. Health Edco WRS Group, 1991. Videocassette.

National Clearinghouse for Alcohol and Drug Information (NCADI), Center for Substance Abuse Prevention. *Drugs of Abuse*. NCADI Publication No. RP0926. Rockville, MD: NCADI, 1998.

National Clearinghouse for Alcohol and Drug Information. *Straight Facts About Drugs and Alcohol*. Rockville, MD: NCADI, 1998.

National Institute on Drug Abuse (NIDA). *Mind Over Matter: The Brain's Response to Stimulants*. NIH Publication No. 97-3857. Rockville, MD: NIDA, 1997.

Sheets, Mark. *Quitting Meth: Your Personal Recovery Plan*. Center City, MN: Hazelden Publishing, 1997.

Spence, W. R. *Stimulants: Running on Borrowed Time*. Waco, TX: Health Edco WRS Group, Inc., 1991.

Syndistar, Inc. *Methamphetamines: Under the Ice*. 18 min. Syndistar, Inc., 1997. Videocassette.

FIND OUT MORE ABOUT AMPHETAMINES AND DRUG ABUSE

The following list includes agencies, organizations, and websites that provide information about amphetamines and other drugs. You can also find out where to go for help with a drug problem.

Many national organizations have local chapters listed in your phone directory. Look under "Drug Abuse and Addiction" to find resources in your area.

Agencies and Organizations in the United States

American Council for Drug Education
164 West 74th Street
New York, NY 10023
212-758-8060
800-488-DRUG (3784)
http://www.acde.org/
wlittlefield@phoenixhouse.org

Center for Substance Abuse Treatment
Information and Treatment Referral Hotline
11426-28 Rockville Pike, Suite 410
Rockville, MD 20852
800-662-HELP (4357)

Eden Children's Project
1035 Franklin Avenue East
Minneapolis, MN 55404
612-874-9441

Marin Institute for the Prevention of Alcohol and Other Drug Problems
24 Belvedere Street
San Rafael, CA 94901
415-456-5692

Narcotics Anonymous (NA)
P.O. Box 9999
Van Nuys, CA 91409
818-773-9999

National Clearinghouse for Alcohol and Drug Information (NCADI)
P.O. Box 2345
Rockville, MD 20847-2345
800-729-6686
800-487-4889 TDD
800-HI-WALLY (449-2559, Children's Line)
http://www.health.org/

National Council on Alcoholism and Drug Dependence
12 West 21st Street, 7th Floor
New York, NY 10010
800-622-2255

National Families in Action
2296 Henderson Mill Road, Suite 300
Atlanta, GA 30345
404-934-6364

Office of National Drug Control Policy
750 17th Street, N.W., 8th Floor
Washington, DC 20503
http://www.whitehousedrugpolicy.gov/
ondcp@ncjrs.org
888-395-NDCP (6327)

Parents' Resource Institute for Education (PRIDE)
3610 DeKalb Technology Parkway, Suite 105
Atlanta, GA 30340
770-458-9900
http://www.prideusa.org/

Shalom, Inc.
311 South Jumper Street
Room 900
Philadelphia, PA 19107
215-546-3470

Agencies and Organizations in Canada

Addictions Foundation of Manitoba
1031 Portage Avenue
Winnipeg, Manitoba R3G 0R8
204-944-6277
http://www.mbnet.mb.ca/crm/health/afm.html

Addiction Research Foundation (ARF)
33 Russell Street
Toronto, Ontario M5S 2S1
416-595-6100
800-463-6273 in Ontario

Alberta Alcohol and Drug Abuse Commission
10909 Jasper Avenue, 6th Floor
Edmonton, Alberta T5J 3M9
http://www.gov.ab.ca/aadac/

British Columbia Prevention Resource Centre
96 East Broadway, Suite 211
Vancouver, British Columbia V5T 1V6
604-874-8452
800-663-1880 in British Columbia

**Canadian Centre
    on Substance Abuse**
75 Albert Street, Suite 300
Ottawa, Ontario K1P 5E7
613-235-4048
http://www.ccsa.ca/

**Ontario Healthy Communities
    Central Office**
180 Dundas Street West, Suite 1900
Toronto, Ontario M5G 1Z8
416-408-4841
http://www.opc.on.ca/ohcc/

**Saskatchewan Health
    Resource Centre**
T.C. Douglas Building
3475 Albert Street
Regina, Saskatchewan S4S 6X6
306-787-3090

Websites

**Avery Smartcat's Facts &
    Research on Children
    Facing Drugs**
http://www.averysmartcat.com/druginfo.htm

**D.A.R.E. (Drug Abuse
    Resistance Education)
    for Kids**
http://www.dare-america.com/index2.htm

**Elks Drug Awareness
    Resource Center**
http://www.elks.org/drugs/

Join Together Online
http://www.jointogether.org/sa/

**National Institute on Drug
    Abuse (NIDA)**
http://www.nida.nih.gov

**Partnership for a Drug-Free
    America**
http://www.drugfreeamerica.org/

Reality Check
http://www.health.org/reality/

**Substance Abuse and
    Mental Health Services
    Administration (SAMHSA)**
http://www.samhsa.gov

**U.S. Department of Education
    Safe and Drug-Free Schools
    Program**
http://inet.ed.gov/offices/OESE/SDFS

**U.S. Department of Justice
    Kids' Page**
http://www.usdoj.gov/kidspage/

D espite what you may have heard, selling illegal drugs will not make you rich. In 1998, two professors, Steven Levitt from the University of Chicago and Sudhir Venkatesh from Harvard University, released a study of how drug gangs make and distribute money. To get accurate information, Venkatesh actually lived with a drug gang in a midwestern city.

You may be surprised to find out that the average street dealer makes just about $3 an hour. You'd make more money working at McDonald's! Still think drug-dealing is a cool way to make money? What other after-school jobs carry the risk of going to prison or dying in the street from a gunshot wound?

Drug-dealing is illegal, and it kills people. If you're thinking of selling drugs or you know someone who is, ask yourself this question: is $3 an hour worth dying for or being imprisoned?

WHAT A DRUG GANG MAKES IN A MONTH*

	During a Gang War	No Gang War
INCOME (money coming in)	$ 44,500	$ 58,900
Other income (including dues and blackmail money)	10,000	18,000
TOTAL INCOME	**$ 54,500**	**$ 76,900**
EXPENSES (money paid out)		
Cost of drugs sold	$ 11,300	$ 12,800
Wages for officers and street pushers	25,600	37,600
Weapons	3,000	1,600
Tributes (fees) paid to central gang	5,800	5,900
Funeral and other expenses	10,300	4,200
TOTAL EXPENSES	**$ 56,000**	**$ 62,100**
TOTAL INCOME	$ 54,000	$ 76,900
MINUS TOTAL EXPENSES	- 56,000	- 62,100
TOTAL AMOUNT OF PROFIT IN ONE MONTH	**- 1,500**	**14,800**

* adapted from "Greedy Bosses," *Forbes*, August 24, 1998, p. 53. Source: Levitt and Venkatesh

Picture Credits

LINDA BAYER has an Ed.D. from the Graduate School of Education at Harvard University and a Ph.D. in humanities. Dr. Bayer has worked with patients suffering from substance abuse and other problems at Judge Baker Guidance Center and within the Boston public school system. She served on the faculties of several universities, including the Hebrew University in Israel, where she occupied the Sam and Ayala Zacks Chair and was twice a writer in residence in Jerusalem.

Dr. Bayer was also a newspaper editor and syndicated columnist, winning a Simon Rockower Award for excellence in journalism. She is the author of hundreds of articles, and is working on a fourth book. She is currently a speechwriter and strategic analyst at the White House, where she has written for a number of public figures, including General Colin Powell and President Bill Clinton.

Dr. Bayer is the mother of two children, Lev and Ilana.

BARRY R. McCAFFREY is director of the Office of National Drug Control Policy (ONDCP) at the White House and a member of President Bill Clinton's cabinet. Before taking this job, General McCaffrey was an officer in the U.S. Army. He led the famous "left hook" maneuver of Operation Desert Storm that helped the United States win the Persian Gulf War.

STEVEN L. JAFFE, M.D., received his psychiatry training at Harvard University and the Massachusetts Mental Health Center and his child psychiatry training at Emory University. He has been editor of the *Newsletter of the American Academy of Child and Adolescent Psychiatry* and chairman of the Continuing Education Committee of the Georgia Psychiatric Physicians' Association. Dr. Jaffe is professor of child and adolescent psychiatry at Emory University. He is also clinical professor of psychiatry at Morehouse School of Medicine, and the director of Adolescent Substance Abuse Programs at Charter Peachford Hospital in Atlanta, Georgia.